Eugene F. Douglass, MS, MDiv, PhD

A Simple Guide to Understanding the Bible

I. Introduction

1. What is hermeneutics?

Hermeneutics is the science that teaches us how to derive the

intended meaning from a passage of writing. It involves principles,

laws, and different methods of interpretation. Sacred Hermeneutics

deals with the interpretation of the Bible as The Inspired Word of

God. Divine inspiration must be maintained, otherwise the Bible

becomes like just another Book.

2. Why is Sacred Hermeneutics necessary?

Because Sin has corrupted the understanding of man,

therefore, great effort must be used to guard against error. The

meaning of the passage must not be distorted by preconceived

notions, presuppositions, denominational doctrine or confessions of

faith. If it is distorted in this way, the study can become a self-serving search for proof texts and not a search for doctrine or the intended meaning from Scripture. Sacred Hermeneutics is also described as Biblical Interpretation.

3. What does Biblical Interpretation involve?

Biblical Interpretation involves Exegesis and Synthesis to gain an understanding of the passage and then Exposition and Application to put the meaning of the passage into a contemporary context. For example, in Luke 24:27 Jesus opened up the meaning of the scriptures written by Moses and The Prophets concerning Himself to the disciples. He enabled them to understand the Scriptures, with the power of The Holy Spirit. The Holy Spirit is He who opens up the Word of God, so we can clearly understand it. A study of Biblical Interpretation gives us tools that the Holy Spirit can use to give us a deeper understanding of God's Word. The Holy Spirit is the vital connector, one who is not a Christian and not indwellt by The Holy Spirit is likely to have faulty interpretation of God's Word. Therefore, a Christian is likely to interpret Scripture better, than a non-Christian Theologian, or even a "Christian" Theologian who does not believe in The Inspired Word. Even one who grew up in the Church can have faulty interpretation because of a lack of a personal relationship with God.

4. The Significance of a Sound Theory of Interpretation.

Proper interpretation is ammunition that confronts issues that divide The True Church of Christ from pretenders and heretics (Mormons, Islam, Jehovah's Witnesses, etc.). It also confronts issues that divide denominations Orthodox, Catholic, Lutheran, and different Protestant groups. Although, as long as Sin remains a problem, certain issues that divide the Church into denominations will never be resolved. Therefore, the only TRUE confession of faith is The Word of God, not constructions of man. Confessions of faith are useful, but cannot be used as foundations for Biblical Interpretation; the Bible must always fill that role.

5. The Preacher/Teacher as Interpreter.

Anyone who preaches or teaches the Word of God (all Christians) is called upon to interpret the Word of God correctly. First of all, He must apply it to himself, and then show his audience how to apply it. In the Old Testament the Levitical Priesthood had that responsibility (Malachi 2:5-7 and Nehemiah 8:1-8). Beginning with New Testament times with the abolition of the priesthood, all Christians have the responsibility to apply the Word of God to their lives and then teach it.

6. The Interpreter's Spiritual Condition.

Ezra 7:10 describes Ezra as a Man of God who knew His Word well, and practiced it in his own life. Teaching the Word of God requires understanding and understanding requires practicing what is learned. Those who preach the Word of God must understand it and therefore, they must live it out themselves. This involves a growing Christian faith, continued sanctification by The Holy Spirit, and a life that becomes more and more Christ-like. The practicers understand it, therefore they can teach it.

II. The Object of Sacred Hermeneutics

1. The Bible, the Inspired Word of God.

The object of Sacred Hermeneutics is The Holy Bible, the inspired Word of God. It is God's direct and special revelation to man, his creation. It is His communication to us in human language that we need to hear Him and to do what He, the Lord, asks of us. 2 Timothy 3:16-17 expresses very clearly that The Word of God is God breathed; God's Word sent to us, to correct us, rebuke us and train us in righteousness. Inspiration involves non-contradiction, clarity, coherence, consistency, truthfulness and freedom from error in what it teaches. For Jesus Christ himself said many times "It is written" meaning God says, or I say. This is additional proof that the written word is Inspired; God breathed. Also, the Word is God's word as Jesus Christ in referred to in John 1 as the Word become flesh.

2. God used human authors to write his word.

Our Sovereign God used human authors to write His Word. They wrote what needed to be written as gave them the Words and enabled them to remember accurately events (John 14:26). Their written words, as we have them, are the Words of God to mankind.

God used their idiosyncrasies, character, intellect, temperament, talents, education, likes, dislikes, and biases as tools to write the necessary words.

3. God as Personal, Immanent, and Omnipotent Author.

God being a personal, immanent, and omnipotent God, He has the power to keep His Word accurate in its teaching, truthful in its history, and consistent in its content. Therefore, The Word of God is inerrant in what it teaches to man today. Because it is God's Word, this implies Unity in the Bible, God's self revelation.

4. The Unity and Diversity of The Bible.

The Bible is the product of The Holy Spirit, the books center on or point to Jesus Christ and His eventual return. Man's Fall, and Christ's redemption are all intertwined in all the Books of The Bible. The progressive nature of God's revelation, his longsuffering, his faithfulness all point to the Redeemer Jesus Christ. Old Testament passages xplained in The New Testament give additional and different meanings, not readily apparent in the Old Testament, serve to unify scripture. The Diversity of The Bible as to content, form, language, historical narrative, laws and commandments, prophesy, and poetry is clear. These all serve to point aspects of God's Character and Man's relationship with God serve to unify The Bible. The diversity brings more unity.

5. Unity in the Sense of Scripture.

There is unity in the Sense of Scripture, therefore it can be investigated scientifically, logically and coherently and that sense is spiritually discerned. God uses unequivocal language to say what needs to be said without misleading us. God's purpose is the Redemption of His Creation through Jesus Christ. God's basis is that He created us so we can understand his rational revelation. God uses perfectly the language of Man to express with clarity what we need to understand. This Unity is encompassed in Jesus Christ as The Word (The Logos) who became man and dwelt among us.

III. Exegesis - General Hermeneutical Principles.

Grammatico-historical Interpretation.

Exegesis - gather from the scriptures themselves the precise meaning that the writer (God) intends to convey. The necessary presupposition, to interpret the scriptures properly is, God has written His Word through human authors, whose use of language expresses the common linguistic conventions and literary forms of their day. Some basic rules for Exegesis are:

1. Interpret words according to use.

2. Interpret sentences according to context.

3. Interpret literary units according to genre.

4. Interpret books according to their historical context.

1. Interpret words according to use.

Lexical Semantics - The Study of words.

1) Etymology - The study of roots or origins of the word. It

is the study of the development of the word to its first known use and compare it, to its use in the sentence. One analyzes it, comparing it to the same word or idea in other languages. The problem with this kind of study is it may give some hints as to its meaning, but may not tell much about its current use. For example, in English the word "nice" comes from the Latin word "nescius" which means ignorant. That is very different from the current meaning "pleasant". The word must also be studied using real roots not logical roots from the English. For example, "eucharist" comes from the Greek word "eucharistia" which means thanksgiving. Some split it up, eu for good, charist for caress or touch from the latin "carus". This is faulty etymology.

Because of these difficulties etymology has limited benefit. It is better to study how the words are used, in its immediate context, in other places in the book, in other books by the same author, by other authors, extra-biblical sources and are there Old Testament concepts for the New Testament word. Various tools for this kind of study are Greek and Hebrew lexicons, parallel lexicons to compare languages and classical lexicons which give uses in extra-biblical sources.

2) Polysemy - Different meanings from them same form.

For example, in English the word "wind", written, can mean a rush of air, or can mean to wind up a clock. These are two different meanings for the same four letters, one is a noun and one is a verb. The meaning would have to be determined by context. Greek and Hebrew have many forms which have different meanings in different context. In Hebrew "davar" can mean thing or matter, in a different context it can mean word, or speech. The key is context.

3) Syntax - The relationship of words in a sentence.

The relationship of words used in a sentence can shed light on the meaning of words. The sentence structure, the grammar, the verb forms, tenses, moods, voices, number all play an important role. Using grammars parsing of the words may be done to bring out the meaning in that context.

4) Figures of Speech.

The use of words in a sentence to give directed meaning.

They are a normal and natural way to communicate forcefully ideas.

     a. Metaphor - a comparison by direct assertion and used as a creative force in language. Most metaphors are designed to make a direct comparison. In Isaiah 1:8-10 Egypt and Babylon are used as metaphors of a lace of bondage or evil place. In Luke 22:31 Jesus says Peter will be sifted as wheat. Elsewhere, suffering is referred to as a refiner's fire or as a cross we must bear.

     b. Simile - An explicitly stated comparison using like or as. For example, in Luke 10:3, Jesus sends his disciples forth as "lambs in the midst of wolves". In a simile, that which follows "like" or "as" is usually a commonly known experience.

     c. Synecdoche - A part representing the whole, or a whole representing the part. For example, "Tickle the ivories" means play the piano. In John 3:22 Jesus is baptizing, yet in 4:1 he is described as not baptizing, as his disciples are doing it.

d. Metonymy - Using the name of one thing to
describe something else. For example, The Body of Christ
for The Church or The White House referring to the
President.

e. Personification - A thing, quality, or idea is
represented by a person. For example, "Therefore do not
worry about tomorrow, for tomorrow will worry about
itself." (Matthew 6:34) In Psalm 114 the Red Sea is described
as fleeing, the Jordan turns back and the mountains skip like
rams.

f. Apostrophe - Words are expressed in an
exclamatory tone to an actual person. The presence or
absence of the person is unimportant. As in David's lament
over his son Absalom in II Samuel 18:33 where he cries "O
my son Absalom, my son, my son, my son Absalom..."

g. Ellipsis - An idea not fully expressed, so the reader must supply the rest of the words to get the idea. Usually the idea is implied in the context, so it is simple to provide the subject or the verbs.

h. Euphemism - A word or phrase is substituted because the direct form of the Word is too harsh, or offensive. For example, "sleep" is used for "death", "to know" is used for sexual intercourse. In Acts 1:25 Luke describes Judas as going down to "his own" place, they tone it down. The language is direct enough to be clear, but it does not offend.

i. Meiois - A negative statement is used to declare an affirmative truth. For example, Jesus' words in Acts 1:5, "You will be baptized with the Holy Spirit not long after these days." In Thess. 2:15-16 the Jews are described as "not pleasing God", that means they anger God.

j. Hyperbole - A conscious exaggeration for effect, a

rhetorical overstatement. For example, in I Kings 10:27, numbers are exaggerated for effect and in verse 26 they are detailed. Hyperbole is also a relative concept described in absolute terms. In Luke 14:26, Jesus says we must hate our father and mother in comparison to Him.

    k. Irony - To express something other than or the exact opposite of the literal meaning for effect. There are three types of irony:

    1) Rhetorical - Fools for Christ

    2) Sarcasm - Irony intended to hurt. For example, 2 Samuel 6:20 Michal, David's wife, mocks him for his spectacle of dancing in the streets.

    3) Satire - Intended to get a point across in a mocking way. For example, in Matthew 23 Jesus Pharisees "White washed tombs" and "blind guides".

2. Interpret sentences according to context.

This can be done by language analysis. The sentence structure, grammatical forms and syntax are all important. There are many grammatical aids for this purpose

 The most helpful of all is discourse analysis. Using the concrete

expression of an idea in a specific context. The discourse can be,

historical narrative, prose, poetry, prophesy, laws and geneologies.

For example, In John 9:3 Jesus said "Neither this man nor his parents

sinned", this must be interpreted within its context. Jesus does not

say He never ever sinned. He is explaining that neither he nor his

parents' sinned to cause his blindness from birth. One can

legitimately say that the Bible says "Commit adultery" and yet it

does not mean that, that must be taken in context. That context is

"You shall not commit adultery." That is quite a different meaning.

Two types of extended figures of speech are used in The

Bible. Extended figures of speech are combinations of sentences to

prove a point or illustrate a concept. These are:

a. Parables - Parables are an extended simile (a comparison,

using like or as) used to illustrate a concept. The parable of the

Prodigal Son in Luke 15:11-32 is to teach us how God will respond

to us, if we reject Him and then when we run back to Him. He will

welcome us and celebrate our return. Jesus used parables to teach

spiritual truths; They illustrate the reign of God, the demands of

God, the love of God, the forgiveness of God, the patience of God,

His mercy, and other similar attributes. Parables are a major part of

the Gospels. The source of the imagery was everyday life and the

settings were those the hearers could relate to. They were purposed

to illustrate the keys to the gospel and encourage people to respond.

b. Allegories - An allegory is an extended form of the

metaphor. In John 10:1-16 The good shepherd represents Christ, the

sheep are those he gave his life for and the flock is His Church. Paul

uses an allegory in Galatians 4:21-31. He gives the story of Hagar,

Ishmael, Sarah and Isaac and gives it new significance. Hagar as the

slave represents the Old Covenant. Sarah represents the New

Covenant. The child of Hagar was born through the flesh, the child

of Sarah is the child of promise. He extends the story to teach

something much more significant, and not addressed in the original

text.

3. Interpret Literary Units according to Genre.

The Bible is literature and therefore can be analyzed as

literature using regular methods. Although, one must not forget it is

the Inspired Word of God. The psalms are to be read as poetry or songs, otherwise they lose some significance. The Bible is not unique in its forms, but its content. The purposes of Language in Scripture are to: inform, command, illuminate, perform (like a play) and celebrate. These are done using three main styles: Narrative, Poetry and Prophesy.

a. Narrative - This is mainly historical, telling of people involved in all shorts of situations. Some examples are, the story of Noah, Adam and Eve, Jonah, Daniel in the Lion's Den and many more. The narratives are to enable us to experience what they experienced, see what they saw and more. This is for the purpose of understanding how God dealt with them, what He taught them, thereby we can learn from their mistakes and see things from God's perspective. Particularly, in how He expects us to behave.

b. Poetry - The psalms are the major portion of poetry in The Bible. They illustrate and highlight the longings of the human soul for forgiveness, deliverance, and redemption. They also praise God for His works, His Gifts, His promises, His attributes and His wisdom. Poetry in Hebrew is used as emphasis and to focus more intently on a subject. Most of the poetry is very graphic in its imagery.

c. Prophesy - Prophesy is God speaking to His people through a man about their spiritual condition, and what is to come. It is used as a warning and also to present promises. The language is pointed, blunt, and they are filled with distinct imagery. This imagery can be very bleak, very brutal, even savage and crude. Yet, its intent is to shock the people of God into action, repentance or to give them hope. Old Testament prophesy largely is warnings about the coming judgment, the New Testament in Revelation the concentration is on deliverance, judgment and Christ's return.

4. Interpret Books According to their Historical Context.

The Bible books must be interpreted with an understanding of the cultural context of when they were written, historical reasons for why they were written and the cultural mindset of those they were written to. In interpreting them it is necessary to ask these questions: "What did the author have in mind?", "What issues of the day was he addressing and Why?," How should these books be understood in their historical settings?" One must explore the

Political, Social, Spiritual, Cultural, Geographical, Ethical and

Technological environments of Israel and her neighbors at the time

the Books were written.

IV. Theological Interpretation

This is referred to as "Special Hermeneutics" and it has distinctive

principles of Hermeneutics in light of the uniqueness of The Bible.

A. The Unity of Scripture

1. The Theme of the whole Bible

The theme of the whole Bible is Man's problem (Sin) and

God's solution, Jesus Christ. God's authorship and direction towards

the final Redemption guarantees its theological unity. The major

themes in the Bible are the creation, the fall, redemption and

judgement. These all point to God and are the backdrop of every

biblical text. In this unity there are a series of Covenants (Formal

Promises He makes to His people), which are Adamic, Noahic,

Abrahamic, Mosaic, Davidic and the New Covenant through Jesus

Christ. Each book addresses one or more of these covenants and knits them into the unity of the whole.

2. The History of Redemption

There is a distinct development of revelation throughout redemption. God shed the blood of animals, and clothed Adam and Eve after they sinned. They were promised that in the future the seed of woman would crush the serpent. This was the first messianic prophesy. The more God revealed to man over time the more He expected of them. At certain levels of revelation God allowed certain things polygamy, the taking of concubines and various customs of the day. As God's revelation expanded these were no longer allowed, He expected more of His People. The is an epochal structure of Biblical History, with a certain level of revelation to those points and then we take this structure and place it in the context of the complete revelation of The Bible. For example, Abraham had a son by Hagar and God blessed Abraham and allowed it. Abraham was still referred to as believing God; although in the light of the whole revelation of scripture now, we see his family did suffer the consequences of his sin. In light of the Whole Bible, the story of David and Goliath is not just heroism, but it shows the

significance of Kingship with God's Authority. David was the

redeemer for Israel, as His seed Jesus was the redeemer for all

mankind. Progressively revelation and redemption move hand in

hand throughout the Bible. This results in the final redemption by

Christ on the Cross, and His resurrection and ultimately the final

judgment.

B. The Relationship between The Old and The New Testaments.

1. Typology - Parallels between the Old and The New Testaments.

This relationship can be discussed in terms of Typology.

Typology is the spiritual relationships between persons, institutions,

offices, and events within the history of redemption, between the Old

and New Testaments. The essential relationship is a promise and its

fulfillment, or a sign post and the destination between the two

Testaments. Therefore, New Testament authors have referred again

and again to the Old Testament Scriptures to show Christ's

fulfillment.

a. Ceremonial Types - Divinely purposed and redemptive enactment of future truth. An Old Testament ritual (for example, the Passover), symbolizes what Christ did in the future (His sacrifice on the Cross). The lamb of Passover, and the Lamb of God are both sacrifices. In Leviticus 16:10 on the Day of Atonement the scapegoat assumed all the people's sins, Jesus is our scapegoat.

b. Institutional Types - The divine purpose of the institution of the High Priest was the mediator between the People and God, only the High Priest could enter the Holy of Holies. Whereas, in the New Testament Jesus Christ becomes our High Priest in a higher order, the order of Melchizedek, as direct intercessor as in Hebrews 4:14, 15, & 7:27. He approaches the Father on our behalf.

c. Historical Types - Hosea in 11:1 describes Israel being called out of Egypt and of bondage by God, this is fulfilled in Matthew 2:15, when the baby Jesus is called out of Egypt to return home to Israel. Jonah in Jonah 1-4 is in the belly of the whale for three days, fulfilled by Jesus for three days in the tomb.

2. The New Testament Use of the Old Testament

The New Testament uses the Old Testament in a variety of

ways:

a. Apologetically - In Psalm 16:10 where it refers to the resurrection and God's Holy One will not see decay. With the fulfillment described in Acts 26:22, 23 by Paul.

b. Prophetic - Joel describes the Coming Day of The Lord in Joel 2:28-32. In Acts 2:17-21 is it repeated for the fulfillment.

c. Typological - In I Cor. 10:1-13 Paul uses a warning from Israel's History not to grumble, as their forefathers did in the wilderness.

d. Theological - In Hebrews 3:1-6 is described how Jesus is greater than Moses.

e. Practical - In I Cor. 9:9 Paul quotes Deut. 25:4 to show that pastors should be paid.

C. The Use of Scripture to Interpret Scripture

There is a fundamental hermeneutical principle that Scripture is its own interpreter. This presupposes the unity of scripture, the inerrancy, consistency, coherence, and the sole authority of the scriptures in matters of faith and practice.

1. Interpret obscure passages in the light of the clear

passages. For example, certain portions of Revelation need to be interpreted in the light of other more clear "last days" passages. Using portions of Daniel, Ezekiel, Matthew 24, I Thessalonians and other passages the meaning of the symbolism will become clearer. Luke 12:40 becomes clearer using I Thess. 5:2 and Rev. 3:3 to back it up. Scripture clarifies scripture.

2. Interpret Individual passages in harmony with the rule of faith. The rule of faith refers to central areas of Christian Doctrine drawn from the clear areas of scripture, where the specific subject matter is dealt with. This means one would not interpret Scripture in such a way that would deny the Deity of Christ, nor the humanity of Christ. However, this principle followed too literally can result in continued error, because confessions of faith are written by men and as such are fallible. Scripture must always be the authority not a statement of faith.

3. Interpret Scripture as a whole, in the light of all its parts. This means we do not take one portion of scripture and act on it without consulting the whole Bible on that issue, to look for additional guidance.

4. Interpret Scripture regulations in light of the principal

behind them.

For example in Matthew 19:3-9 Jesus is addressing the issue of divorce, but discusses the principal behind the prohibition "Two shall become One flesh", but divorce was only allowed because of the hardness of man's heart. The hardness of man's heart leads to adultery and the resulting divorce. It does not make divorce acceptable.

5. Interpret historical in light of the didactic. The didactic can protect from over emphasis on a historical passage. The didactic sets the constraints. Acts 18 mentions Priscilla as a leader in the church and a woman of God and then say I Timothy 3 when it gives the leadership to men only is therefore wrong. Women can serve in the church other women and children, Acts 18 does not bless the ordination of women.

6. Interpret the Old Testament in light of the New Testament. For example, Romans 4 in the New Testament will help us understand the story of Abraham in Genesis 12-23 and God's promise of the land to him.

D. The Use of Logic in Biblical Interpretation.

The Bible is the Word of God in what it expresses directly and by what is logically deduced from it. The language of the Bible suggests important truths that are imbedded in the words. This is why the parables of our Lord are so clear, they encourage logical, rational thought on the part of the hearers to receive the full meaning. The parable of the Prodigal son if Jesus told it only for a literal, strict interpretation, would only apply to a man who gets his inheritance and squanders it and returns humbled and is received warmly, because he returned. That is all, the rest of the message comes from logical deduction of the extended simile. Men when they write can say things between the lines they do not intend to say, but God being perfect will have only that between the lines be consistent with clear scripture. No doctrine should come from only between the lines, it therefore would not be consistent with God's clearly revealed Word. For example, the Roman Catholic Church interpreted Scripture in such a way as to prove that all the heavenly bodies revolved around the earth. Therefore, Galileo was excommunicated because scientific investigation proved that the earth and the planets revolved around the Sun. Their interpretation was faulty because of their Aristotlian presuppositions. Their presuppositions colored how they interpreted between the lines, and the result was not confirmed with a clear passage, so it was condemned to fail. If we let scripture interpret scripture by putting implied scripture to the light of clear scripture, more error can be avoided. No truth implied in scripture will contradict a clear truth in scripture.

V. Contemporary Application of Scripture.

A. The Scriptures must be applied according to their due and proper proportion.

The more important truths are central. In Matthew 22:37-40 Jesus states the two commandments, that all the law hangs on. You shall have no other Gods before me, and Love your neighbor as yourself. The penalty for adultery was death, the penalty for stealing was restitution, the proportion is very clear.

B. Apply Scripture according to its generic sense.

The meaning of scripture in its context must be applied, and no accommodation of the language of Scripture is allowed. For example, saying "No, it really doesn't mean that!" when it obviously does is wrong. Those "Christians" that say a homosexual marriage or union is acceptable are dead wrong. This is why constant bible study is important, so we can build a reservoir of understanding and wisdom that the Holy Spirit can draw as we apply it to our lives. Romans 15:4 states, The Bible was written to teach us, so we can be encouraged in our walk. I Cor. 10:11 states the Bible is full of examples and warnings to teach and train us.

C. Apply Scripture to situations that are genuinely parallel.

In Matthew 4:5-7 Satan perverts scripture to tempt Jesus and Jesus responds with scripture directly applicable to the situation. Satan tempts him to jump "God will protect you", Jesus responds "You shall not put the Lord your God to the test." Obviously, the scripture Satan was using was not applicable to the situation Jesus was in, Satan perverted scriptures for his own ends. Jesus got it back on course, with an appropriate scripture. There are two types of parallels:

1. Redemptive - Historical Parallels

For example, circumcision for the people of Israel in Old Testament times to represent the Covenant. The New Covenant brought a circumcision of the heart.

     2. Cultural and Moral laws, encompassed in ceremonial and civil law or customs.

Some cultural traditions were a holy kiss, foot washing, or that respectable women did not braid their hair. These would not necessarily be applicable for today. Some actions or rules are all custom, others are from principles that transcend culture, and some are a combination. The interpreter (hopefully filled with The Holy Spirit) must decide.

Conclusion:

Interpreting Scripture can be challenging, rewarding and enjoyable as long as some central concepts are not forgotten:

1. The Bible is the Inspired Word of God not merely a book.
2. The Holy Spirit is the true interpreter of Scripture, His work in

the life of a Christian can guard him from error. The Holy Spirit's

Illumination is vital for proper interpretation. Without Him, much of

The Bible will be foolishness.

3. Apply the Word of God to your life. This gives us true

understanding of God's Word so we can share it with others. One

cannot possibly properly interpret the scriptures, if his life does not

glorify God.

THE END

I used the above methods to develop my own Statement of Faith,

regarding what I believe as a Christian. That Statement of Faith

serves as Part 2.

Bibliography:

Berkhof, Louis; "Principles of Biblical Interpretation",
Baker, Grand Rapids, MI Copyright 1950

Ryken, Leland; "How to Read the Bible as Literature",
Academie, Grand Rapids, MI Copyright 1984 Zondervan

Stuart, Douglas; "Old Testament Exegesis", Westminster,
Philadelphia, PA Copyright 1984

Fee, Gordon D.; "New Testament Exegesis", Westminster,
Philadelphia, PA Copyright 1983

Mickelson, A. Berkeley; "Interpreting the Bible", Eerdmans,
Grand Rapids, MI Copyright 1963

Holmes, Arthur F.; "All Truth is God's Truth", Eerdmans,
Grand Rapids, MI Copyright 1977

Part 2 - Statement of Faith

Eugene F. Douglass

Spring 1989 M. Div.,

Bethel Theological Seminary

West Campus, San Diego, CA

This is an example as to how I interpret the Bible,
using passages to describe my beliefs as a Christian.

Integrating Motif

My statement of faith will use as the integrating motif "The Grace of God". I chose this motif because it is the grace of God which has saved me, and the grace of God which has been forming my doctrine and transforming my mind.

The grace of God is vital for all that I believe, because only with that grace am I capable of believing it. That may sound silly or trite, but it is very important for me. For without the grace of God, I would not be finishing seminary, but in jail, in a mental hospital or dead. Who knows how bad things would have gotten, if I was able

to resist the call of God in my life on March 11, 1973.

The grace of God has been revealed to man, in God's creation

(general revelation), and in His Word (contained in the Old and New

Testaments, this is special revelation). By God's grace all God's

elect (The Church) are saved. And by His grace we can live our new

life with Him. It is God's grace that enables me to believe and say

for myself "I have been crucified with Christ, it is no longer I who

live but Christ who lives in me, and the life which I now live, I live

in the faith of the son of God, who loved me and gave His Life for

me". (Galatians 2:20)

God's Grace Revealed to Man

1. Special Revelation

a. The Bible

I believe the Holy Bible to be the only sufficient,

certain and infallible rule of all saving faith. I believe

the Holy Bible was inerrant in the original autographs

(originally written in Hebrew, Aramaic and Greek), and so

is faithful regarding the historical record, and any other things it presents as factual. I believe in things scientific it is accurate and without error, but it is not a scientific textbook with much detail, but only what is important for the readers to know. The Bible contains the totality of what we are to believe concerning God, and gives us guidance on what He expects of us. (2 Tim. 3:15-17, Isa. 8:20, Romans 15:4)

I believe the Bible consists of the Old and New Testaments in 66 books. Those commonly called "The Apocrypha" are not part of the canon and are not of divine inspiration, with no authority to the church of God. (Luke 24:27,44)

The authority comes from God the Author, and depends not on the testimony of any man or church, but stands on its own because it is the Word of God. (1 Thess. 2:13, 1 John 5:9)

My full persuasion and assurance of the infallible truth and the divine authority thereof, is from the inward work of the Holy Spirit bearing witness to and with the Word in my heart. (1 Cor. 2:10-12)

I believe it contains the whole counsel of God concerning all things necessary for his own glory, man's salvation, faith and life in Him, is either clearly written down, or contained in the Bible, unto which nothing at any time is to be added, whether by "new" revelation of the Spirit, or traditions of men. The Holy Spirit illuminates my heart so I can understand the diverse portions of scripture and apply them to life, and my life in particular. (Gal. 1:8,9, John 6:45)

I believe the most important rule of interpretation of scripture is the scripture itself, so when any question is not evident about the true and full sense of the passage, the Bible must be searched for places that speak more clearly, and by that clear meaning can the unclear passage be understood. (2 Peter 1:20,21, Acts 28:23)

b. The Nature of God and The Trinity

I believe the Lord Our God is one living and true God, He created all things visible and invisible, and is himself not created, but without beginning or end. He is spirit, without body, immortal, true light, immutable, immense, eternal, incomprehensible, almighty, infinite, holy, wise, free, absolute, works all things as He wishes for His Own glory, loving, gracious, merciful, long-suffering, good and true, forgiving, just, wrathful against the ungodly, hating all sin and He will judge the guilty. He has dominion over all His Creation, and can do as He pleases with all of it. (Deut. 6:4, Jer. 10:10, Ex. 3:14, John 4:24, I Tim. 1:17, Mal. 3:6, I Kings 8:27, Jer. 23:23, Ps. 90:2, 95:3, Prov. 16:4, Rom. 11:36, Ex. 34:6,7, Heb. 11:6, Neh. 9:32,33, Nah. 1:2,3, Rev. 5:12-14)

I believe in God there are three persons, The Father, The Son (or The Word), and The Holy Spirit, all of one substance, power and eternity, each having the whole divine essence, yet the essence undivided.

1. The Father - The Father is not created, nor does

He has a beginning, nor is He proceeding, and He directs

the Son and The Holy Spirit to do His will.

2. The Son - Eternally Begotten of the Father to do

His will, and to give His Life as a ransom for many.

3. The Holy Spirit - The Holy Spirit proceeding from

the Father and The Son to do their will, to the Glory of

God.

c. God's decree.

I believe that God has decreed all things that will

or have come to pass; yet is not the author of sin, and

allows His creation varying degrees of free will, according

to His pleasure so all are accountable to Him for their

actions. I believe by this decree that some men and angels

are predestined or foreordained to eternal life, through

the sacrifice of Jesus Christ, who died to save the world

from the penalty of sin, and the others are left to act in

their sin, to receive their just condemnation to show His

justice before His elect. The number of His elect cannot

be increased nor diminished, and those are predestined from

before the foundations of the World. (Isa. 46:10, Eph.

1:11, James 1:13,17, John 19:11, Eph. 1:3-5, Rom. 8:30,

9:11-18, 22,23, 2 Tim. 2:19, John 6:44, 2 Peter 1:10).

2. General Revelation

God's general revelation is in His creation, that man

can observe and study. It pleased the Triune God to create

all things for His Glory alone, and so He reveals Himself

through all of it. He created all things in six time

periods, and on the seventh he rested and all He created is

very good. God created man, male and female in His image

for His glory, with reasonable and immortal souls enabling

them to live their lives as God had designed for them, the

Law of God written on their hearts, and yet able to do or

go contrary to the Father's will (this free will existed

only in Adam and Eve before the fall). After the fall, the

general revelation of God is still evident, and acts enough

so, none are without excuse, and yet is easily misunderstood

by those who have not received the special revelation from

God. (Jon 1:1,5, Heb. 1:2, Romans 1:20, Col. 1:16, Gen.

1:26-28, 2:1,2,7, Rom. 2:14,15)

3. God's Provision for Man

a. Divine Providence

I believe God upholds, directs, orders, all creatures

and things, from the least to the greatest, to the end for

which they were created. God provides the first cause, and

so, all things happen according to His will, so there is

nothing that happens by chance or due to luck. Yet, He has

things occur, as second causes. God is not the primary

cause of many events, but does have them happen using

others as agents, to have His Will be done. In the fall,

the sinfulness of their acts proceeds only from them, and

not from God who neither is or can be the author of Sin.

Often in God's providence we may be left to experience the

consequences of our sin, to teach us, or humble us, so that

we may become more dependent on God and His provision to

conquer sin in our lives, and to teach us to be careful

lest we fall again. Whatever comes upon His elect is by

His desire that we might learn from it and grow in our walk

with Him. And whatever comes upon the unbeliever is due to

His own sinfulness, and whom he serves, as the devil

destroys his own. (Heb. 1:3, Isa. 46:10,11, Ps. 13:5,6,

Matt. 10:26-33, Eph. 1:11, 2 Cor. 12:7-9, Romans 8:28,

1:24-32, 2 Thess. 2:10-12)

b. The Fall of Man

I believe God created man sinless, and perfect,

without blemish or stain, and gave him a righteous law

which would have resulted in eternal life, had he kept it,

and yet man did not abide long in this honor, Satan using

the subtle serpent to seduce Eve to disobey God's law, and

then she seduced Adam, who, without any compulsion chose

to

disobey the clear edict of God by eating of the forbidden

fruit. These our first parents fell from their elevated

state, and death came upon them and all their descendants,

all becoming spiritually dead in their sins. The guilt of

Adam's sin was imputed to all his offspring, the corrupted

nature taking a greater toll with each succeeding

generation, unless the pattern is broken by one becoming a

Christian. From this original corruption we are rendered

unable to please God, and wholly inclined to do evil, and

as such all transgressions proceed from this original

corruption. We can only be freed from this corruption by

the imputed righteousness of Jesus Christ upon those who

believe. (Gen. 2:16,17, 3:12,13, Rom. 3:23, 5:12-19, Titus

1:15, Jer. 17:9, Rom. 3:10-19, 6:12,20, 7:18,23-25, 8:7,

James 1:14,15, Gal. 5:17)

c. God's covenant

I believe God, knowing the state into which man had

fallen, provided a way out through which man might be saved

from his deserved condemnation, and this way out is through

Jesus Christ alone. He covenanted with His people, that by

the shedding of blood, man could be saved. The shedding of

animal's blood covered (temporarily) their sin, and pointed

to the once for all sacrifice of Jesus Christ to truly

cleanse from all sin. This covenant is a covenant of Grace

and Mercy, where He freely offers all mankind eternal life

and forgiveness of sins by Jesus Christ. He, then requires

faith in Him so that they might be saved. He, then

provides for all who believe, the Holy Spirit so they can

now have the power to live their lives to glorify God in

every way. This covenant was revealed first to Adam, with

its fulfillment in the gospels, in the sacrifice of Jesus

Christ on the cross to save the elect from their deserved

condemnation. (Luke 17:10, Gen. 3:17, Rom. 8:3, John 3:16,

John 6:44,45, Gen. 3:15, Heb. 1:1, 2 Tim. 1:9, Titus 1:2,

Heb.11:6,13, Acts 4:12)

God's Graceful Provision - Christ and Salvation

4. Christ the Mediator

I believe that God chose and ordained the Lord Jesus

Christ, His Only Son, to be the only mediator between God

and man. He is prophet, priest, and king, head and savior

of his church, the heir of all things, and judge of the world. God gave Him a people to be His seed, and to be by Him redeemed, called, justified, sanctified and glorified. (Is. 42:1, Acts 3:22, Hebrews 5:5,6, Luke 1:33, Eph. 1:23, Acts 17:31, Is. 53:10)

I believe the Son of God became man, conceived by the Holy Spirit, born of the Virgin Mary, with two whole, perfect and distinct natures, which were inseparably joined together in one person; which person is God and Man, the only mediator between God and Man. He lived a life of total obedience to the Father's will. He underwent the punishment due to us with his stripes and sacrifice on the cross. He died for the sins of His elect, saw no corruption, and on the third day rose again from the dead. He appeared to His disciples, and then ascended into heaven. He is now sitting at the right hand of the Father making intercession for us before Him, and shall return at the end of the age, to judge men and angels. (John 1:14, Rom. 8:3, Heb. 2:14-17, 4:15, Luke 1:27-35, 1 Tim. 2:5, Acts 10:38, Heb. 7:26, John 5:22,27, Heb. 10:5-10, Gal.

3:13, 2 Cor. 5:21, Matt. 27:46, 1 Cor. 15:3,4, John

20:25,27, Acts 1:9-11, Rom. 8:34, 14:9,10, 3:25,26, Heb.

9:15, John 16:8)

5. Free Will

I believe that man was originally created with the

freedom to choose good or evil, in his state of innocence.

He was capable of choosing good or evil, but with his fall

from this state of innocence lost any ability to choose any

spiritual good. So, man as being unregenerate is unable to

convert himself or prepare himself for fellowship with God

by his own strength. When God converts a sinner, the man

is freed from his bondage to sin and again is enabled to do

that which is pleasing to God, and yet man is unable to be

flawless in doing good until glorification. (James 1:14,

Ecc. 7:29, Gen. 3:6, Rom. 5:6, Eph. 2:1,5, Titus 3:3-5,

John 6:44, 8:36, Philippians 2:13, Rom. 7:15-23, Eph. 4:13)

6. Salvation, Sanctification and Glorification

a. Effectual Calling

I believe those whom God has predestined to eternal life, will in His time be called by His Word and Spirit, out of a state of sin and death to Grace and Salvation through Jesus Christ. Their minds are enlightened to understand the things of God, their wills renewed, and by His Power determining them to be drawn to Jesus Christ, willingly and freely responding to His Grace. This calling is by God's own choice, and is not due to any merit or power in the man who responds. By this calling the man is enabled to respond, by his new free will, to the gift of God, of eternal life. I believe this calling includes elect infants, imbeciles, and others who are incapable of being outwardly called by the Word of God, according to God's good pleasure. I believe that all those who die in infancy, or before the age of accountability are subject to the will of God, whether they are elect or not. I believe there is biblical precedent to say that the children of an elect parent is also elect. I believe those not elected, cannot respond to the gospel, and so are lost forever.

(Rom. 8:30, 11:7, Eph. 2:1-6, Acts 26:18, Eph. 1:19, 2 Tim. 1:9, Eph. 2:8, 1 Cor. 2:14, John 3:3-6, 6:44,45,65, Acts 4:12)

b. Justification

I believe for those God effectually calls, He also justifies by pardoning their sins, and accepts them as righteous. This is not because of what they did, but for Christ's sake alone. Jesus Christ's obedience to the whole law fulfilled the requirements of the Law, and so we can receive His righteousness by Faith as a gift from God. Faith in the sacrifice Christ made for me, taking my sins upon Himself, and dying in my place, is what justifies me. I believe that it is Faith in the sacrifice to come that saves the Old Testament saints, believing in the promises given in God's word to them for a future redeemer. (Rom. 3:24,28, 4:5-8, 1 Cor. 1:30,31, Rom. 5:17-19, Eph. 2:8-10, John 1:12, Isa. 53:5,6, Gal. 3:8, Titus 3:4-7, Rom. 4:22-24, Gen. 3:15, 22:1-14, Ex. 12:1-30)

c. Adoption

I believe that with all who are justified, God makes them joint heirs with Jesus Christ. They have become true children of God, and as such are cared for, and inherit the promises, one of which is eternal life. We become His children, and can claim the name "Children of God", whereas before we were children of Satan, and God did not know us. (Eph. 1:5, Gal. 4:4,5, John 1:12, Rom. 8:15-17, 2 Cor. 6:18, 1 Peter 5:7, Heb. 12:6)

d. Sanctification

I believe for those God has adopted, He starts the process of sanctification, which molds us, and transforms us into the image of Jesus Christ. Sinful areas of life are conquered, and brought under the power of The Holy Spirit, and the mind is transformed, so we can walk more and more in patient obedience to God's will for our lives. The unregenerate portion of man diminishes, and the regenerate increases, and this process continues until glorification, when we are removed from this prison of our earthly bodies, and take on the new one God has designed

for us. (Acts 20:32, Rom. 6:5,6, Eph. 3:16-19, Rom. 6:14,

2 Cor. 7:1)

e. Saving Faith

I believe that saving faith for the elect, is the work

of the Holy Spirit in their hearts, through the Word of God

preached to them. This faith is increased and strengthened

through baptism, the lord's supper, prayer and various

other means. By this faith, we believe that the Word of

God is true and trustworthy, and that it tells us what we

are to believe, and what God expects of us. By this saving

faith we receive all the promises of God to us, as new

creatures in Christ Jesus. (2 Cor. 4:13, Rom. 10:14,17,

Luke 17:5, Acts 24:14, Ps. 19:7-10, 2 Tim. 1:12, Heb.

11:13, Gal. 2:20, Heb. 5:13,14)

f. Repentance

I believe that for those who are saved, they have

repented unto life. They have turned from their life of

sin, and asked God to transform them to live their lives to

glorify God. This repentance unto life can come at any

time in a man's life, either as a child, or when he is old,

the turning is still real, and shows its effect in the

man's life. This repentance involves humbling, godly

sorrow, detestation of the sin, praying for pardon and

strength, with a new purpose to live one's life to please

God. It is all men's duty to repent of known particular

sins, as God reveals them to him, and so cooperate in their

sanctification. This repentance continues throughout life,

and plays a great part in sanctification of the believer.

(Titus 3:2-5, Acts 11:18, Ez. 36:31, 1 Tim. 1:13-15, Isa.

1:16-18)

g. Good Works

I believe that truly good works are only those which

God has commanded in His word, these good works done in

obedience to God's Word are the fruits and evidence of a

true and lively faith, and by them believers thank God for

what He has done for them. These good works do NOT save

us, or help us earn eternal life, as that is a gift of

God in response to our faith. The good works of

unbelievers, that on the surface may seem to be what God

commands, and have "good" results apparent to all are

sinful and cannot please God, because they proceed from a

heart still tainted with sin. (Micah 6:8, Heb. 13:21,

James 2:18-22, 1 John 2:3-5, 2 Peter 1:5-11. Matt. 5:16,

Eph. 2:8-10, John 15:4,5, Matt. 25:21-23, Heb. 11:4-6,

Titus 3:5, Matt. 25:41-43)

h. Perseverance of the Saints

     I believe that those saved, will NOT lose their

salvation, and this perseverance does not depend on their

own free will, but upon the immutability of their election.

One who is truly saved, will evidence that saving faith, by

his perseverance. Those who appear to be saved, and then

fall away, have been revealed as not truly having saving

faith to begin with. I believe that some may have the hand

of God on their lives, and not truly respond until later,

but may appear to repent and fall, repent and fall, until

they receive the true power to live their lives to glorify

God. I believe a true Christian is not capable of (or will

not continue in) grievous sin (such as adultery,

homosexuality, drunkenness, moral turpitude) as a lifestyle

as 1 Cor. 6:9-10 clearly states they will NOT inherit the

kingdom of God. Verse 11 clearly states that new life in

Christ transforms people, so they will not do such anymore.

(John 10:28,29, Philippians 1:6, 1 John 2:19, Rom. 8:30,

Heb. 6:17,18, 1 John 3:9, Jer. 32:40, 1 John 2:3-6, 1 Cor.

6:9-11)

i. Assurance

I believe through the doctrine of perseverance of the

believer, that the true Christian can have, by the

believing of the above promises from God's word, true and

total assurance that God has saved him, made him new, and

is in process of transforming him to the image of Chris

Jesus. This assurance is infallible, as it is based on the

sacrifice Christ paid for us, by giving up His life in our
place, the inward evidences of God's working in our hearts,
and the testimony of the Holy Spirit that we have been made
children of God for good! New and weak Christians may
suffer from doubts, but that is due to a heart of unbelief,
that will not believe the clear teaching of scripture.
Some may doubt, because of persons that teach that one can
lose their salvation, and that doubt is man-made. (1 John
2:3-6, 3:14-24, 5:13, Rom. 5:1-5, Heb. 6:17,18, 2 Peter
1:4,5,10,11, Rom. 8:15,16, 1 John 3:1-3)

j. The Gospel and the Extent of Grace Thereof

   I believe the Gospel of Jesus Christ, which is special
revelation, is the only means by which man can be saved.
General Revelation is not enough to lead one to the
knowledge of the truth. The revelation of the gospel to
sinners, has been under the sovereign will of God, to go,
and reach peoples as He alone ordains. The Holy Spirit
works through the Word of God and its proclamation to save
the man whom God has predestined to be saved. And it can

happen no other way. Plainly those in nations not reached

by the gospel, cannot be saved, as they are under the curse

of God, as all are without excuse, being offspring of Adam,

the first sinner. (Rom. 10:14-17, Isa. 60:2,3, Acts 16:7,

Rom. 1:18, 1 Cor. 2:14, John 6:44, 2 Cor. 4:4-6)

The Grace of God in His Church and in His Return

7. Christian Liberty

I believe the liberty that we have as Christians

consists in the freedom from the guilt of sin, the wrath of

God, and the curse of the Law, and in deliverance from the

forces of darkness that run rampant in this world. We have

free access to God, and decide to obey our Lord, because it

pleases Him. We have also been freed from the ceremonial

law which bound the Jews, as Jesus Christ fulfilled it.

(Gal. 3:13, 1:4, Acts 26:18, Rom. 8:3,28, 1 Cor. 15:54-57,

1 John 4:18, Heb. 10:19-21)

I believe that God alone is Lord of the conscience,

and so, Laws of man that are contrary to His Word, do not

bind me, likewise any that are not contained in it. (Rom.

14:4, Matt. 15:9, Col. 2:20-23) And this liberty is not a

liberty to go on sinning, but a liberty to freely choose

what is right and honorable. (Rom. 14:4, Matt. 15:19, Col.

2:20-23, Rom. 6:1,2)

8. Christian Marriage

I believe marriage is an institution designed by God

to illustrate the union between Christ and His Bride the

Church, it is to be between one man and one woman, with no

bigamy or adultery on either's part. It was designed for

the mutual help of husband and wife, for the bearing of

children, and for prevention of immorality. I believe

Christians must marry only Christians, as marrying with an

unbeliever is becoming unequally yoked with the world, and

those that do it, will reap much more than that they sowed.

I believe Christian marriage must not be incestuous, nor

have any basis in immorality on the part of either one.

(Eph. 5:22-33, Gen. 2:24, Matt. 19:5,6, Gen. 2:18, I Cor.

7:2,9, Neh. 13:25-27, 1 Cor. 5:1)

9.The Nature of the Church

a. What is the Church?

I believe in one catholic or universal church, which

by the work of The Holy Spirit may be called invisible, and

consists of the whole number of the elect, that have been,

are or will be gathered into one, under Christ, the True

Head, and is the bride of Christ, the body, and the

fullness of Him that makes us all one in Him. (Hebrews

12:23, Col. 1:18, Eph. 1:10,22,23, Eph. 5:23,27,32)

I believe that all persons throughout the world

professing the faith of the gospel of Jesus Christ, and

obedience unto God by their life in Christ, are and may be

called the visible saints (I Cor. 1:2, Acts 11:26); and of

these people all particular congregations are constituted

(Romans 1:7, Eph. 1:20-22)

I believe that the purest churches in this world are

subject to mixture and error (I Cor. 5, Rev. 2&3); and some

have so degenerated as to become churches not of Christ

(Rev. 18:2, 2 Thess. 2:11,12), but gatherings of the
people of Satan, but in spite of all this, Christ always
has had, and ever shall have a kingdom in this world (Matt.
16:18, Ps. 72:17, 102:28, Rev. 12:17), to the end of this
world, of such as believe in Him, and make a profession of
His name.

I believe that The Lord Jesus Christ is the one True
Head of His church, and there can be none other. There is
no one representative of Him on earth. (Col. 1:18, Matt.
28:18-20, Eph. 4:11,12, 2 Thess. 2:2-9)

I believe in that God has instituted local churches
for the preaching and teaching of the Word, the edification
of believers, the propagation of the gospel, and the
fellowship of the believers. (John 10:16, 12:32, Matt.
18:15-20, 28:20)

I believe the members of these churches are saints
(Rom. 1:7, I Cor. 1:2), visible to all in the world,
showing people with their lives, what they confess is true.
(Acts 2:41,42, 5:13,14, I Cor. 4:13).

b. Church Government

I believe in a particular church so gathered, and
completely organized according to the Will of God, consists
of officers and members: and the officers appointed by
Christ, to be chosen and set apart by the church, so called
and gathered, for the specific administration of
ordinances, and the execution of power or duty, which He
calls them to or trusts them with, are bishops or elders
and deacons. (Acts 20:17,28, Philippians. 1:1, Titus 1, I
Tim. 3)

I believe the way appointed by Christ for the calling
of any man, fitted and gifted by the Holy Spirit, unto the
office of elder or deacon in a church is chosen by the
members of the church itself (Acts 14:23) and solemnly set
apart by fasting and prayer, with the laying on of hands by
the eldership of the church. (I Tim. 4:14, Acts 6:3,5,6)

I believe the deacons and elders of the church are to
be men, above reproach, only once married (if married, I
Cor. 7 indicates that Paul may not have been married), not

divorced and who manage their family well, and no woman is to preach, teach or have spiritual authority over men, but content themselves with the God given extremely important roles of ministering to other women and children. (1 Tim 2:10-16, Titus 1, I Tim. 3, I Pet. 3:1-7)

I believe the work of pastors is to teach, preach, counsel, equip and confront the people of God, and the world with the Gospel of Jesus Christ, and with the Word of God, with what God expects of us, as Christians, and challenging the unsaved elect, with the good news of Jesus Christ, that can save man from his sin. (Acts 6:4, Heb. 13:17, Ez. 3) It is the responsibility of the churches to whom they minister, not only to give them all due respect, but also, to pay them responsibly, according to their ability, so the minister will live comfortably, without themselves being caught up in secular affairs. (I Tim. 5:17-18, Gal. 6:6-7, 2 Tim. 2:4, 1 Tim. 3:2, I Cor.9:6,14)

I believe however it the responsibility of all believers to share their faith with their neighbors both in their words and actions. And so, we are all ministers and

priests to those who need help. (Acts 11:19-21, I Pet.

4:10,11)

c. Communion of Saints

I believe it is the responsibility of all believers to

unite themselves with a local body of believers, when and

where they have opportunity to do so, for nurture,

fellowship, and correction; so all are admitted unto the

privileges, censures, and government of a church according

to the rule of Christ. (I Thess. 5:14, II Thess. 3:6,14,15)

I believe in cases of difficulty or differences,

either in point of doctrine or administration; wherein

either the churches in general are concerned or any one

church, or any member or members of the churches are

affected in censures not agreeable to truth and order, it

is appropriate for messengers of like churches to meet and

consider and give their advice in this matter, and report

the result to all the churches concerned that the matter

might be resolved. These messengers however do not have

the authority or power to exact discipline or impose their

determination on any involved. As this is the

responsibility of the local church. (Acts

15:2,4,6,22,23,25, 2 Cor. 1:24, I John 1:4)

10. The Ordinances

a. Baptism

I believe Baptism is an ordinance of the New

Testament, ordained by Jesus Christ, to be done to the new

believer, as a sign of his new fellowship with him in his

death and resurrection (Rom. 6:3-5, Col. 2:12, Gal. 3:27);

of his being united with Christ; of forgiveness of sins

(Mark 1:4, Acts 26:16); and of his giving up unto God,

through Jesus Christ, to live and walk in newness of life.

(Rom. 6:4)

I believe the only ones who actually profess

repentance towards God, faith in and obedience to our Lord

Jesus Christ, are the proper subjects for Christian

baptism.

I believe if practiced on an infant, it only can serve
as an infant dedication to the Lord for His service, and
does not save, nor is it a new circumcision replacing the
old act of circumcision.

I believe the fluid to be used in baptism is water, in
the name of The Father, The Son and The Holy Spirit (Matt.
28:19,20, Acts 8:38).

I believe the proper way to baptize is to immerse or
dip the person in water (Matt. 3:16, John 3:23).

b. The Lord's Supper

I believe the supper of the Lord Jesus, was instituted
by Him, on the same night that He was betrayed, to be
observed in His churches unto the end of the world, for the
perpetual remembrance and showing forth the sacrifice of
Himself in His death, and serves as confirmation of the
faith of believers in all the benefits thereof (I Cor.
11:23-26), their spiritual nourishment and growth in Him,
their further obedience to Him, and to be a pledge of their
communion with Him, and with each other (I Cor.
10:16,17,21).

I believe the Lord's supper is only a memorial to the sacrifice Christ offered on the cross for us once for all, and is not a repeated sacrifice of the body and blood of Christ. (Heb. 9:25,26,28, I Cor. 11:24, Matt. 26:26,27).

I believe the Lord Jesus has in this ordinance appointed His ministers to pray, and bless the elements of bread and wine (or grape juice), and by this sets them apart for a holy use, and to take and break the bread and to take the cup and give both to the communicants (I Cor. 11:23-26).

I believe that the elements remain in substance both bread and wine, and they remain as they were before (I Cor. 11:26-28).

I believe that worthy receivers outwardly partaking of the visible elements of bread and wine, do then also inwardly, by faith, spiritually and to an unknown degree physically receive and feed upon Christ crucified and all the benefits of his death (I Cor. 10:16, 11:23-26): the body and blood of Christ, under, with and in and spiritually present in the elements.

I believe because of the above that anyone who partakes of communion with unrepentant sin brings judgment upon himself that can lead to sickness or even death. (I Cor. 11:29) I believe that if there was no real presence physically or spiritually, and it was just a memory, this scripture would be effectively disarmed.

11. The State of Man after death/resurrection

I believe that the bodies of men after death return to dust from which they were made (Gen. 3:19); but their souls, which neither die nor sleep, are immortal, and immediately enter the presence of God if they are Christians, or into Hades if they are not Christians as they wait for the Last Judgement, and the resurrection of the body. The godly are comforted in this state (Ecc. 12:7, Luke 16:19-31, Luke 16:25).

12. The Second Coming, Tribulation/Millennium

I believe the second coming of the Lord is both

imminent and impending, and will occur when we least expect

it. Whatever the millennial view we have, the return of

Christ is not dependent on what we believe, but what God

makes clear in His word. (Mark 13:35-37, Luke 12:35,36,

Rev. 22:20)

I believe the second coming to be post-tribulational,

and if there is a millennium, pre-millennial. (Matt.

24:22) This verse does not promise removal from the

tribulation, but shortening for the sake of the elect. I

believe the scripture describing the rapture, describes the

dead in Christ rising and those still alive will be

transformed, and meet Christ in the air. I believe the

second coming describes both a coming with His people, and

a coming for His people. (1 Thess. 4:11-17)

I believe that there will no be a millennium as the

only direct evidence for a millennium found in Rev. 20, is

symbolic, using 1000 years to describe our eternal reign

with Jesus Christ, because it is a perfect number 10x10x10.

However, if I there is a millennium, I don't know what the

situation will be like. There seems to be some inherent

contradictions in this concept. "Why would we have incorruptible bodies on a corrupted earth?" is just one example.

I believe at the Last day, those of the saints who are alive on the earth shall not die or sleep but be changed (I Cor.15:51,52, I Thess. 4:17) and the dead shall be raised up with incorruptible physical bodies, and shall be united with their souls forever. (Job 19:26,27, I Cor. 15:42,43)

I believe the bodies of the ungodly shall be raised again, to dishonor; the bodies of the godly raised to honor and made conformable to Christ's body, by His power and might (Acts 24:15, John 5:28,29, Philip. 3:21)

13. The Last Judgement

I believe that God has appointed a day where He will judge the world in righteousness by Jesus Christ, in that day all angels, and all people shall appear before Jesus Christ to give account of their thoughts, words and deeds, and to receive according to what they have done in the body, whether good or evil (Acts 17:31, John 5:22,27, I Cor. 6:3, Jude 6, 2 Cor. 5:10, Ecc. 12:14, Matt. 12:36, 25:32, Romans 14:10,12).

I believe at the end of this judgement day, there will be the manifestation of His glory of His Mercy, in the eternal salvation of the elect; and of His justice, in the eternal damnation of the non-elect (Rom. 9:22,23). The righteous shall go into eternal life, and receive their reward, in the presence of the Lord, but the wicked shall be cast into eternal torments and punished with everlasting destruction, away from the presence of the Lord. (Matt. 25:21,23,34,46, 2 Tim. 5:8, Mark 9:48, 2 Thess. 1:7-11)

I believe that the ungodly will be sent to a place of eternal torment, with no chance of it ending. It is described in many ways, unquenchable fire (Matt. 5:22, 18:8-9), destruction (Matt. 10:28), everlasting torment (Matt. 13:41-42), wrath (John 3:36), lake of fire and sulfur (Rev. 20:10,14,15, 21:8). Each man will suffer in hell what He deserves (Luke 12:47-48).

14. The New Heavens and the New Earth

I believe that on the day of judgment God will

destroy and remake or renew the heavens and the earth to be

incorruptible, without blemish and pure. Heaven and Earth

will no longer be separated but be in the presence of each

other (Rev. 21:1-3). I believe that finally man will be

able to fulfill his calling described in Gen. 1:28, to fill

and subdue the earth without sin. There will be a new

heaven and a new earth this is clear (Is. 65:17, Rev.

21:1), but whether it is renewed or remade is really

unimportant. It will be new, we will dwell there, and in

the presence of the Lord Jesus (Rev. 21:1-4), and the

peoples of the earth will dwell together in unity, with no

tears or hurts (Rev. 22:1-5)

Bibliography

Adapted and personalized from The Philadelphia Confession of Faith of 1742 Copyright 1981 Grace Abounding Ministries, Sterling, VA pgs. 1-147. A wonderful Baptist statement of faith, originally adapted from The London Confession of Faith of 1689, and the Westminster Confession of Faith of 1644

Hoekema, Anthony A. The Bible and The Future Eerdmans, Grand Rapids, MI Copyright 1979 The whole book.